John. [from old catalog] Jenkins

Catalogue of the Wesleyan Female College

1860-1861

John. [from old catalog] Jenkins

Catalogue of the Wesleyan Female College
1860-1861

ISBN/EAN: 9783744650533

Printed in Europe, USA, Canada, Australia, Japan

Cover: Foto ©Andreas Hilbeck / pixelio.de

More available books at **www.hansebooks.com**

CATALOGUE

OF THE

TRUSTEES, FACULTY, AND STUDENTS

OF THE

Wesleyan Female College,

MACON, GEORGIA,

1860--1861.

MACON, GEORGIA:
JOHN L. JENKINS, BOOK AND JOB PRINTER.
1861.

Board of Trustees.

3

Board of Instruction.

Rev. JOHN M. BONNELL, A. M.,
PRESIDENT,
PROFESSOR OF MENTAL AND MORAL SCIENCE AND RHETORIC.

Rev. COSBY W. SMITH, A. M.,
PROFESSOR OF MATHEMATICS.

Rev. FRANCIS X. FORSTER, A. M.,
PROFESSOR OF ANCIENT LANGUAGES.

Rev. WILLIAM C. BASS, A. M.,
PROFESSOR OF NATURAL SCIENCE.

Mons. C. SCHWARTZ,
PROFESSOR OF MODERN LANGUAGES AND DRAWING, AND ASSISTANT IN MATHEMATICS.

Miss MARY E. CARLTON,
ASSISTANT IN LITERARY DEPARTMENT.

Miss C. M. SEMPLE,
PRINCIPAL PREPARATORY DEPARTMENT.

P. G. GUTTENBERGER,
SENIOR PROFESSOR OF MUSIC.

W. S. B. MATTHEWS,
JUNIOR PROFESSOR OF MUSIC.

Miss LOUISA GUTTENBERGER,
ASSISTANT IN MUSIC.

Miss M. A. MATTHEWS,
ASSISTANT IN MUSIC.

Madame SOPHIE SCHWARTZ,
INSTRUCTRESS IN ORNAMENTAL NEEDLE-WORK, &C.

HADDAM P. REDDING and LADY,..........*Steward's Department.*

Mrs. E. J. STEPHENS,....................................*Matron.*

W. C. BASS,..*Secretary.*
C. W. SMITH,...*Librarian.*
C. SCHWARTZ,..*Accountant.*

☞ All remittances of money or communications relating to financial matters must be addressed to the Accountant; for Catalogues and Circulars, to the Secretary; on all other matters, to the President.

4

ALUMNÆ.*

1 8 4 0 .

Miss CATHARINE E. BREWER,
" SARAH V. CLOPTON,†
" ELIZABETH FLOURNOY,
" ANN E. HARDEMAN,†
" MARTHA F. HEARD,
" JULIA M. HEARD,

MISS SARAH M. HOLT,
" MATILDA J. MOORE,
" HARRIET M. ROSS,
" MARY L. ROSS.
" MARGARET A. SPEER.

1 8 4 1 .

MISS ADELINE BREWER,
" ELIZABETH BRIDGES,
" MARY CALDWELL,
" CAROLINE CHILDERS,
" SARAH E. CHILDERS,†
" CATHARINE L. DREWRY,
" SARAH J. FLINT,†
" MARY ANN HAMILTON,
" SARAH M. JAMESON,
" ANN LE CONTE,

MISS MARY H. MARSH,
" JULIA MARSH,
" ANN E. MIMS,
" SUSAN J. MYRICK,
" ANN V. PARIS,
" MARY C. POWELL,†
" JUVERNIA ROSE,†
" AMELIA C. SNIDER,
" TABITHA WHITE,†
" ANN MARIA WINN.†

1 8 4 2 .

Miss MARY E. BURKHALTER,
" ELIZA W. COTTON,†
" ELIZABETH S. DOWDELL,
" ANN E. FLUKER,
" HARRIET L. HAMILTON,

MISS PAULINA V. HARDEMAN,
" AMANDA J. HINES,
" MARTHA E. LIGON,
" MARY E. RICHARDS,
" JULIA A. THARPE.

* THE ALUMNÆ of the GEORGIA FEMALE COLLEGE are included in this Catalogue. In the year 1844 the Institution was re-organized unde. a new name, and the Graduates of subsequent years are Alumnæ of the WESLEYAN FEMALE COLLGE.

†Deceased.

5

1 8 4 3.

Miss Martha Cooper,
" Sarah E. Curd
" Eliza A. Jarvis,

Miss G. A. Merriwether,
" H. E. Shackleford,
" Julia Snider.*

1 8 4 4.

Miss Henrietta Dean,
" Wilhelmina Lanier,
" Eliza A. Martin,*

Miss Margarat D. Martin,
" M. A. McDowell,*
" Harriet A. Scott.

1 8 4 5.

Miss Margaret E. Bailey,*
" Elizabeth Conyers,
" Arabella O. Dean,
" Catharine M. Dowdell,*
" Elizabeth Evans,
" Ann Flewellen,
" Catharine Freeman,
" Martha J. Hardaway,
" Sarah J. Hardeman,

Miss Henrietta S. Hodges,
" Claudia Holmes,*
" Sarah Hudson,
" Geraldine E. Lamar,
" Frances E. Quarles,
" Mary E. Reynolds,
" Ophelia Sanders,*
" Elodia B. Trapp,
" Harriet L. Winn.

1 8 4 6.

Miss Mary A. Anthony,*
" Mary J. Burch,
" Sarah M. Kellum,*
" Eliza A. Gresham,
" Virginia Lindsay,
" Clara C. Pierce,

Miss Anna M. Reynolds,
" Eugenia A. Sanders,
" Minerva A. Spivey,
" L. F. Warren,
" Laura E. Winship.*

1 8 4 7.

Miss Jane E. Bryan,
" Evelina A. Chambers,
" Caroline V. Comer,
" Susan M. Cornwell,
" L. Clifford Cotton,
" Julia A. Flanders,
" Tabitha J. Guyton,
" Sarah E. Hardaway,

Miss Virginia E. Holland,*
" Victoria J. Holmes,*
" Mary S. Howard,
" Sarah E. Myrick,*
" Madaline M. Scott,
" Elizabeth A. Solomon,
" Catharine Wellborn.*

* Deceased.

1 8 4 S .

Miss Ann E. Branham,
" Mary F. Bivins,
" Mary J. Broome,
" Susan E. Ellison,*
" Clara M. Hodges,
" Julia C. Jewett,
" Caroline M. Rawls,*

Miss Sarah S. Posey,
" Mary E. Smith,
" Anna S. Snider,
" Caroline C. Wade,
" Mary E. Walker,
" Mary V. Warren.

1 8 4 9 .

Miss Anna E. Blount,
" Julia Boon, -
" Sarah A. Chapman,
" Julia A. Choat,
" Eliza F. DuPont,
" Helen F. Evans,
" Emily J. Harris,
" Mary Augusta Hill,
" Eliza R. Jones,

Miss Virginia W. Leonard,
" Ann E. Persons,
" Mary B. Quigley,
" Louisa Rogers,
" Joanna E. Shropshire,
" Ann E. Smith,
" Mary A. Taylor,
" Ada J. Tharpe,
" Margaret A. Wade.

1 8 5 0 .

Miss Mary C. Andrew,
" Indiana F. Birch,
" Ann M. Carlton,
" Louisa E. Chapman,
" Mary V. Clarke,
" Martha L. Fort,
" Malinda M. Gamble,
" F. R Guttenberger,
" Louisa E. Harris,
" Georgia A. A. Hill,
" Clara Ella Hill,*
" Anna D. Hutchings,
" Octavia Jones,
" Harriet L. Jones,

Miss Mary A. Jones,
" Sarah M. Lester,
" Sarah A. Lumsden,
" Anna M. Moultrie,
" Ann M. Pitts,
" Charlotte E. Posey,
" T. M. Richards,
" Sarah E. Roberts,
" Georgia A. Rogers,
" Rebecca F. Sasnett,
" C. C. Solomon,
" Acsah E. Sparks,
" Caroline E. Tompkins,
" Annabella J. Tucker,

* Deceased.

1 8 5 1 .

Miss Leona V. Ballard,
" Mary L. Banks,
" Mary S. Bond,
" Georgia A. V. Brinn,
" Ann E. Burkhalter,
" Mary S. Capers,
" Ella G. Clanton.
" Julia M. Davis,
" Octavia J. Douglas,
" Maria J. Easterling,
" Mary A. Evans,
" Susan C. Evans,
" Mary A. Everett,

Miss Mary E. Finn,
" Caroline E. Fort,
" Oceana S. Goodall,
" Mary C. Harris,
" Sarah F. Hines,
" Mary V. Holt.
" Mary A. Jones,
" Rosa Lawton,
" Martha A. Oliver,
" Indiana A. Solomon,
" Tabitha J. Strong,
" Sarah J. Thomas,
" E. M. Williams,

1 8 5 2 .

Miss Octavia O. Andrew,
" Philoclea L. Banks,
" Georgia A. E. Bryan,
" H. P. Burkhalter,
" Mary E. Carlton,
" Mary Ann Cowles,
" Elizabeth S. Dean,
" Mary F. Dean,
" Ann S. Edwards,
" Frances A. Floyd,
" Evelyn A. Harrison,
" F. Augusta Hill,
" Julia H Jones,
" Sarah H. Lythgoe,

Miss C. W. Moultrie,
" Ella C. Pierce,
" Mary F. Rawls,
" Caroline V. Ross.
" T. A. Sapp,
" Sarah L. Simms,
" O. M. Stinson,
" Mary E. Sturges,
" Julia A. D. Thomas,
" Eugenia Tucker,
" Mary M. Tucker,
" Martha F. Williams,
" S. F. Woodruff.

1 8 5 3 .

Miss Mollie A. Anderson,
" Mary E. Atkinson,*
" Sarah A. Bardwell,
" Mary H. Billing,
" Sallie E. Booth,
" Louisa M. Brantly,

Miss Mary F. Burkhalter,
" Martha P. Clements,
" Celestia A. Comer,
" Lillia R. Dowdell,
" Kate Duncan,
" Mary A. DuPont,

* Deceased.

1 8 5 3 , — CONTINUED.

Miss Louisa F. Ellis,
" Ann Franklin,
" Martha B. Hardaway,
" Ovidia L. Hardeman,
" Melissa A. Hill,
" Emma W. Hurt,
" Carrie E. Jones,
" Virginia E. Lestre,

Miss Sallie M. Littlejohn,
" Mary E. Myrick,
" Lizzie Pitts,
" Georgia A. Pope,
" Mary J. Snow,
" Martha F. Solomon,
" Eliza G. Solomons.

1 8 5 4 .

Miss Carrie C. Bennett,
" Fannie L. Chastain,
" Maria L. Comer,
" Marian J. Cotton,
" Harriet A. Hammond.
" Eliza A. Holt,
" Eliza H. Jewett,
" Susan E. Jones,*
" Ann E. Persons,
" Sallie B. Persons,

Miss Julia A. Powell,
" Fannie E. Richardson,*
" Mary A. R. Robinson,
" Mary B. F. Sims,
" Anna E. Simmons,
" Helen G. Simmons,
" Carrie E. Smith,
" Sarah C. Smith,
" Martha J. Stinson.

1 8 5 5 .

Miss M. W. Armstrong,
" Susan Bethune,
" Susan L. Boon,
" Sarah A. N. Burge,
" Mary Ann Crumley,
" Eliza Flewellen,*
" Louisa C. Guyton,
" Ann Eliza Holt,
" Eliza G. Howard,
" Rebecca E. Hurt,

Miss Ann M. Levy.
" Mary E. Luckey,
" Mary A. Lumsden,
" Louisa J. Richards,
" Llizabeth J. Shields,
" Eliza L. Stubbs,
" Helen M. Swearingen,
" Georgia A. Tucker,
" Martha E. Virgin,
" E. Abbie Yopp.

1 8 5 6 .

Miss Elizabeth B. Bellamy,
" Almira Bird,
" Susan E. Bivins,*
" Louisa St. C. Cullens,

Miss Sarah E. Jones,
" Emma Lamkin,
" Anna E. Newton,
" Emily Pou,

* Deceased.

1 8 5 6 , — CONTINUED.

Miss E. V. Garlick,
" Mary E. Groce,
" Rosaline Groce,
" Laura E. Hines,
" Eugenia H. Howard,

Miss Sarah M. Redding,
" Sarah E. Smith,
" Mary B. Walton,
" Sarah G. Yopp,
" M. J. Zitrouer.

1 8 5 7 .

Miss Mary E. Bivins,
" Georgia Conner,
" Virginia Conner,
" Eugenia J. Culler,
" Antoinette Dozier,
" Margaret A. Garlick,
" Catharine V. Griffin,
" Anna R. Gunby,
" Sarah M. Hudson,

Miss Louisa W. Kendall,
" Mary R. Mathis,
" Isabella N. Persons,
" Mary P. Ready,
" Mary E. Rylander,
" Henrietta C. Smith,
" Marietta A. Smith,
" Augusta A. Wardlaw.

1 8 5 8 .

Miss Mary E. Bass,
" Ann S. Bowman,
" Laura E. Butts,
" Sarah A. B. Carver,
" Emma Clark,
" Alice R. Culler,
" Cordelia Dessau,
" Elvira Flewellen,
" Mary E. Fogle,
" Davia Hardeman,
" Martha Hightower,
" Mary Houston,
" Delia Jewett,

Miss Mary F. Jones,
" Susan A. E. Morel,
" Sarah J. Ousley,
" M. Antonia Pettus,
" Sarah A. Phillips,
" Margaret R. Ralston,
" Julia C. Rogers,
" Marion P. Rose,
" Mary E. Rossetter,
" Elizabeth Scott,
" Laura O. Tucker,
" Mary G. Virgin,
" Sarah J. Whitby.

HONORARY SECOND DEGREE.

Mrs. Jane T. H. Cross.

1 8 5 9 .

Miss Rosa M. Anderson,
" Margaret B. Bellamy,
" Mary L. Boon,

Miss Ann E. Collins,
" Elizabeth Crook,
" Mary C. Dixon,

1 8 5 9 , — CONTINUED.

Miss Leda J. Dowdell,
" Julia F. Goode,
" Louisa Guttenberger,
" Martha Harrison,
" Julia Lundie,
" Ella Mason,
" Lucia E. Mulholland,
" Ann Olivia Newton,

Miss Mary S. Norris,
" Sarah F. Paine,
" Mary L. Poole,
" Martha Powell,
" Sarah R. Rogers,
" Sarah E. Taylor,
" Mary L. Whitby,
" Ida Winship.

HONORARY SECOND DEGREE.

Mrs. Susan S. Hancock.

1 8 6 0 .

Miss Mary L. Butts,
" Mary E. Clark,
" Frances J. Coachman,
" Julia M. Dixon,
" Fannie M. Drake,
" Georgia A. Fort,

Miss Emily P. Hightower,
" Elizabeth E. Mims,
" Virginia J. Mims,
" Clara A. S. Smith,
" Loretta J. Virgin.

SECOND DEGREE.

Mrs. Catharine E. Benson,
" Elizabeth Branham,
" Martha F. Bell,
" Julia M. Elder, -
" Sarah M. Ward,
" Matilda J. Brazeal,
" Harriet M. Colquitt,
" Mary L. Grimes,
" Margaret A. Stovall,
" Mary A. Corbin,
Miss Elizabeth Bridges,

" Mary Caldwell,
Mrs. Caroline Swift,
" Catharine L. Comer,
" Mary A. Blackshear,
" Sarah M. Rodgers,
" Ann Stevens,
" Mary H. De Graffenried,
" Julia Patterson,
" Ann E. Lockett,
" Susan J. Williams,
" Ann V. Hill,

SECOND DEGREE,---CONTINUED.

Mrs. Amelia C. Brown,
" Mary E. Carter,
" Elizabeth S. Myrick,
" Ann E. Bloom,
Miss Harriet L. Hamilton,
Mrs. Pauline V. Logan,
" Amanda J. Hobbs,
" Martha E. Clopton,
" Mary E. Knight,
" Julia A. Lundie,.

Miss Martha Cooper,
Mrs. Sarah E. Carhart,
" Eliza A. Ingraham,
" G. A. Bacon,
" H. E. Munnerlyn,
" Henrietta Holt,
" Wilhelmina Eason,
" Marg. D. Lawson.
" Harriet A. Freeman.

Undergraduates.

SENIOR CLASS.

NAMES.	RESIDENCE.	
MISS AMANDA J. BARNETT,	Milledgeville,	Ga.
MISS EMMALA S BELLAMY,	Monticello,	Fla.
MISS M. LUSANNA BURGE,	Newton Co ,	Ga.
MISS CORNELIA E. CARSWELL,	Jefferson Co.,	Ga.
MISS CATHARINE E. CATER,	Vineville,	Ga.
MISS META M. HARBAUM,	Macon,	Ga.
MISS MATTIE HOGE,	Macon,	Ga.
MISS SARAH E. HUDSON,	Jefferson Co.,	Ga.
MISS MARY B. JOHNSON,	Macon	Ga.
MISS FRANCENA S. LOVE,	Talbot Co.,	Ga.
MISS LUDY M. PAINE,	Aberdeen,	Miss.
MISS MARTHA S. ROBERTSON,	Greenville,	Ga.
MISS JOSEPHINE C. RUMPH,	Houston Co.,	Ga.
MISS EUNICE A· RYLANDER,	Sumter Co.	Ga.
MISS E. FLORINE STEVENS,	Walthourville,	Ga.
MISS CAROLINE M. TAYLOR,	Pulaski Co ,	Ga.
MISS KITTY TOOKE,	Houston Co.,	Ga.
MISS OPHELIA C. TUCKER,	Laurens Co ,	Ga.
MISS AMNA M. WILLIAMSON,	Vineville,	Ga.

Undergraduates.

JUNIOR CLASS.

NAMES.	RESIDENCE.	
MISS ELLA E. ANDERSON,	Burke Co.,	Ga.
MISS MILDRED S. BEALL,	Lumpkin,	Ga.
MISS SARAH E. BOON,	Macon,	Ga.
MISS MATTIE A. CATER,	Vineville,	Ga.
MISS MARY E. CHAMBERS,	Columbus,	Ga.
MISS VIRGINIA S. DOZIER,	Muscogee Co.,	Ga.
MISS OCTAVIA J. FENNEL,	Decatur,	Ala.
MISS MARY E. GARNER,	Mobile,	Ala.
MISS SALLIE O. GILMER,	Montgomery,	Ala.
MISS LUCIA GRISWOLD,	Griswoldville,	Ga.
MISS ANNA M. HAMMOND,	Edgefield District,	S. C.
MISS GRETA A. HAMMOND,	Macon,	Ga.
MISS MARY A. HARRIS,	Washington Co.,	Ga.
MISS ELIZA J. HARRISON,	Oxford,	Ga.
MISS GABRIELLA HARRISON,	Macon,	Ga.
MISS MARTHA C. HOLT,	Meriwether Co.,	Ga.
MISS SUSAN A. HOWARD,	Bibb Co.,	Ga.
MISS FLORENCE S. JONES,	Thomas Co.,	Ga.
MISS MARIA V. JULIEN,	Macon,	Ga.
MISS SARAH V. LAMAR,	Macon,	Ga.
MISS LAURA E. LEONARD,	Talbotton,	Ga.
MISS ELLA B. LIPSCOMB,	Athens,	Ga.
MISS VIRGINIA MILLER,	Savannah,	Ga.
MISS MARY PICKETT,	Vineville,	Ga.
MISS ELIZABETH J. REED,	Madison,	Ga.
MISS MARY F. RILEY,	Houston Co.,	Ga.
MISS SUSAN E. ROBISON,	Columbus,	Ga.
MISS MARTHA A. ROSSER,	Eatonton,	Ga.
MISS ANNA E. RUSH,	Talbot Co.,	Ga.
MISS ANNA E. SHEWMAKE,	Burke Co.,	Ga.

14

Undergraduates.

JUNIOR CLASS—CONTINUED.

NAMES.	RESIDENCE.
MISS JULIA B. H. SMITH,	Talbot Co., ... Ga.
MISS MARY P. SMITH,	Decatur Co., ... Ga.
MISS CORA C. SOLOMON,	Twiggs Co., ... Ga.
MISS MARY T. TINDALL,	Macon .... Ga.
MISS JULIA J. TURNBULL,	Monticello .... Fla·
MISS SARAH C. TURRENTINE,	Houston Co., ... Ga.
MISS ELLEN V. TUTOR,	Vineville, ... Ga.

SOPHOMORE CLASS.

NAMES.	RESIDENCE.
MISS EMMA ADAMS,	Eatonton, ... Ga.
MISS CATHARINE C. BENSON,	Bibb Co., ... Ga.
MISS MARY J. BRUTON,	Bainbridge .... Ga.
MISS ANNIE E. CARVER,	Oglethorpe, ... Ga.
MISS EMMA C. CULLER,	Perry, ... Ga.
MISS LILA S. EDWARDS,	Cuthbert, ... Ga.
MISS THEODOSIA H. EVERETT,	Fort Valley, ... Ga.
MISS VIRGINIA C. FINLAYSON,	Jefferson Co., ... Fla.
MISS TEXANNA L, HARDAWAY,	Montgomery, ... Ala.
MISS ANNA HARGROVE,	Vineville, ... Ga.
MISS LOYOLA HARDEMAN,	Tuskaloosa, ... Ala.
MISS M. EVERETT B. HARRIS,	Thomaston, ... Ga.
MISS FLORIDA E. HOLLINGSWORTH,	Macon, ... Ga.
MISS ISADORE HOLLINGSWORTH,	Macon, ... Ga.
MISS MARY L. HOLMES,	Vineville, ... Ga.
MISS SALLIE R. JETER,	Chunnenuggee, ... Ala.
MISS LILLIE A. WILLIAMS,	Meriwether Co., ... Ga.
MISS LAURA L. WIMBERLY,	Twiggs Co., ... Ga.
MISS IRENE C. WOOLFOLK,	Houston Co., ... Ga.

Undergraduates.

SOPHOMORE CLASS—CONTINUED.

NAMES.	RESIDENCE.	
MISS EMMA J. KENNON,	Oxford	Ga.
MISS MARIA J. KILPATRICK,	Concordia Parish,	La.
MISS LIZZIE F. KING,	Decatur Co.,	Ga.
MISS MARY E. LEWIS,	Sparta,	Ga.
MISS MARTHA C. MARSHALL,	Eatonton,	Ga.
MISS JULIA E. MAUND,	Talbot Co.,	Ga.
MISS ELLA R. McKAY	Fort Valley,	Ga.
MISS MARTHA J. MELL,	Macon	Ga.
MISS MARY M. MORRIS,	Macon,	Ga.
MISS MARY H. MUNNERLYN,	Decatur Co.,	Ga.
MISS MARGARET T. MURPHY,	Burke Co.,	Ga.
MISS VIRGINIA A NELSON,	Twiggs Co.,	Ga.
MISS SUSIE S. PERSONS,	Fort Valley,	Ga.
MISS LUCY L. PETTUS,	Monticello,	Fla.
MISS VIRGINIA F. POWELL,	Union Springs,	Ala.
MISS FLORIDA J. REDDING,	Macon	Ga.
MISS SALLIE RICE,	Vineville,	Ga.
MISS SARAH C. ROBERTSON,	Greenville,	Ga.
MISS MARY M. ROSS,	Macon,	Ga.
MISS FANNIE M. SEARCY,	Monroe Co.,	Ga.
MISS MARY L. SHEWMAKE,	Burke Co.,	Ga.
MISS MARY V. SHINHOLSER,	Bibb Co.,	Ga.
MISS ARABELLA L. SLAPPEY,	Houston Co.,	Ga.
MISS MARY E. SLAPPEY,	Houston Co,	Ca
MISS SARAH R. SLAPPEY,	Macon Co.,	Ga.
MISS JULIETTE B. SMITH,	Macon,	Ga.
MISS M. FLORENCE SNIDER,	Savannah,	Ga.
MISS GERTRUDE SNIDER,	Savannah,	Ga.
MISS RACHEL L. SPAIN,	Brooks Co.,	Ga.
MISS TALLULAH M. STUBBS,	Bibb Co.,	Ga.
MISS MARY F. THOMPSON	Thomaston,	Ga.
MISS ADALAIDE M. TUCKER,	St. Landry Parish,	La.
MISS FRANCES E. WADE,	Macon,	Ga.

Undergraduates.

———◆◆◆◆———

SECOND CLASS.

NAMES.	RESIDENCE.
MISS LAURA A. ANDERSON,	Macon, Ga.
MISS VERONICA E. BALL,	Carroll Co., Miss.
MISS MARY E. BATTS,	Washington Co., Ga.
MISS SARAH C. BATTS,	Washington Co., Ga.
MISS FANNIE A. BLOUNT,	Macon, Ga.
MISS ROBA P. BRYAN,	Twiggs Co., Ga.
MISS ANNA A. CHAPMAN,	Twiggs Co., Ga.
MISS CLARA E. CLAPP,	Muscogee Co., Ga.
MISS MARY L. CONE,	Harris Co., Ga.
MISS LOUISA E. CRUTCHFIELD,	Oxford, Ga.
MISS ELLA A. EVANS,	Macon, Ga.
MISS URQUHART EVANS,	Macon, Ga.
MISS JULIA A. EXPERIENCE,	Macon, Ga.
MISS MARY J. GARY,	Shreveport, La.
MISS VALERIA GUNN,	Houston Co., Ga.
MISS MARY A. HEARD,	Augusta, Ga.
MISS ELLA S. KING,	Decatur Co., Ga.
MISS SARAH E. LESTER,	Jones Co., Ga.
MISS ANNIE M. LINTON,	Madison Co., Fla.
MISS SALLIE MEACHAM,	Muscogee Co., Ga.
MISS LUCY McMULLEN,	Macon, Ga
MISS SALLIE E. MOUGHON,	Albany, Ga.
MISS ARCHER R. OGILVIE,	Shreveport, La.
MISS AUGUSTA L. OGILVIE,	Shreveport, La.
MISS MARY W. PAINE,	Aberdeen, Miss.
MISS SARAH PAUL,	Bibb Co., Ga.
MISS FANNIE E. PERKINS,	Tallahassee, Fla.
MISS ELIZABETH M. REYNOLDS,	Cass Co., Ga.
MISS DELIA M. ROBERTS,	Macon Co., Ga.
MISS EMMA M. ROGERS,	Macon, Ga.

17   c

Undergraduates.

SECOND CLASS—CONTINUED.

NAMES.	RESIDENCE.	
MISS WILLENA SHERWOOD,	Macon,	Ga
MISS OLIVE STEPHENS,	Macon,	Ga.
MISS MARY E. STUCKEY,	Darlington District,	S. C.
MISS CALLIE J. SUTLIVE,	Fort Gaines,	Ga.
MISS LIZZIE H. THOMPSON,	Atlanta,	Ga.
MISS JULIA TAYLOR,	Sumter Co.	Ga.
MISS LIZZIE P. TUCKER,	St. Landry Parish,	La.
MISS MOLLIE A. WATTS,	Hancock Co.,	Ga.
MISS ELIZA F. WILLIAMS,	Baker Co.,	Ga.

FIRST CLASS.

NAMES.	RESIDENCE.	
MISS CORNELIA F. ALLEN,	Houston Co.,	Ga.
MISS MARY A. ANDERSON,	Macon,	Ga.
MISS SARAH A. BATTLE,	Monroe Co.,	Ga.
MISS WILLIAM BELLAMY,	Monticello,	Fla.
MISS MARY E. BOWMAN,	Bibb Co.,	Ga.
MISS CLARA B. BURTON,	Ellaville,	Ga.
MISS ELLA L. BURTON,	Ellaville,	Ga.
MISS LAURA CALHOUN,	Houston Co.,	Ga.
MISS HENRIETTA L. CHAIRES,	Leon Co.,	Fla.
MISS MARY E. CHERRY,	Vineville,	Ga.
MISS MATTIE A. CHERRY,	Vineville,	Ga.
MISS S. CORA CLANTON,	Augusta,	Ga.
MISS HENRIETTA L. CLARK,	Albany,	Ga
MISS SUSIE E. CLAYTON,	Wetumpka,	Ala.
MISS ADDIE EVANS,	Russell Co.,	Ala.

Undergraduates.

------◆◆◆------

FIRST CLASS—CONTINUED.

NAMES.	RESIDENCE.
MISS ANNIE P. EVANS,	Russell Co., Ala.
MISS SARAH E. KILPATRICK,	Concordia Parish, La.
MISS VALERIA LAMAR,	Vineville, Ga.
MISS JULIA M. LESTER,	Jones Co., Ga.
MISS ELLA T. LUNDY,	Bibb Co., Ga.
MISS JULIA F. NORRIS,	Baker Co., Ga.
MISS JULIA M. PYLES,	Newnansville, Fla.
MISS JANIE S. REED,	Madison, Ga.
MISS ANNIE D. ROSS,	Macon, Ga.
MISS LEONA H. ROSS,	Macon, Ga.
MISS SOPHRONIA RUSSELL,	Vineville, Ga.
MISS S. CAROLINE SEARCY,	Monroe Co., Ga.
MISS CORINNA SMITH,	Macon, Ga.
MISS FLORA A. SMITH,	Macon. Ga.
MISS MARGARET H. SMITH,	Macon, Ga.
MISS MARY F. SOLOMON,	Vineville, Ga.
MISS CHARLOTTE E. TAYLOR,	Pulaski Co., Ga.
MISS EMMA J. TUCKER,	St. Landry Parish, La.
MISS EMMA G. TURNER,	Lumpkin Co., Ga.
MISS EMMA WARD,	Cuthbert, Ga.
MISS MARY A. WHITTAKER	Bibb Co., Ga

------◆◆◆------

IRREGULARS.

NAMES.	RESIDENCE.
MISS SARAH F. ALLEN,	Macon Co., Ala.
MISS CELESTIA J. COLLIER,	Lexington, Ga.
MISS MARTHA COOK,	Early Co., Ga.

Undergraduates.

IRREGULARS—CONTINUED.

NAMES.	RESIDENCE.
MISS JULIA A. DRANE,	*Taylor Co.,* Ga.
MISS JEMMIE V. GATHINGS,	*Aberdeen,* Miss.
MISS LOUISA E. HAMMOND,	*Macon,* Ga.
MISS MELINDA HUGHES,	*Monroe,* La.
MISS FANNIE R. JOHNSON,	*Holmes Co.,* Miss.
MISS MARY E. LAMKIN,	*Columbia Co.,* Ga.
MISS MARY A. LOVETT,	*Burke Co.,* Ga.
MISS NANCY LOVETT,	*Burke Co.,* Ga.
MISS JULIA F. PELOT,	*Newnansville* Fla.
MISS AMELIA E. SIMPSON,	*Macon,* Ga.
MISS EMMA L. STAPLER,	*Hamilton Co.,* Fla.
MISS LOUISA M. STILES,	*Macon,* Ga.
MISS CLEMENTINA L. STROZIER,	*Albany,* Ga.
MISS EMILY WHITE,	*Chattooga Co.,* Ga.
MISS LAURA M. WILLIAMS,	*Bulloch Co.,* Ga.
MISS MARY W. WILLIAMS,	*Bulloch Co.* Ga.
MISS VIRGINIA St. C. WILLSON,	*Monroe,* La.
MISS MARY E. WYNN,	*Forsyth,* Ga.

PREPARATORY DEPARTMENT.

NAMES.	RESIDENCE.
MISS M. LOUISA BONNELL,	*Macon,* Ga.
MISS REBECCA E. BRYAN,	*Houston Co.,* Ga.
MISS FANNIE T. BURKE,	*Macon,* Ga.
MISS MARY B. BURKE,	*Macon,* Ga.
MISS MARY E. DRAKE,	*Macon,* Ga.

𝔘𝔫𝔡𝔢𝔯𝔤𝔯𝔞𝔡𝔲𝔞𝔱𝔢𝔰.

PREPARATORY DEPARTMENT—CONTINUED.

NAMES.	RESIDENCE.	
MISS E. FLEWELLYN EVANS,	Macon,	Ga.
MISS LOUISA C. FORSTER,	Macon,	Ga.
MISS MARY PARKS,	Macon,	Ga.
MISS MARY V. REYNOLDS,	Cass Co.,	Ga.
MISS MATTIE H. REYNOLDS,	Cass Co.,	Ga.
MISS MATTIE ROSS,	Macon,	Ga.
MISS GERALINE J. RUSSELL,	Vineville,	Ga.
MISS LEILA C. SAULSBURY,	Macon,	Ga.
MISS GEORGIA STEPHENS,	Macon,	Ga.

Ornamental Department.

INSTRUMENTAL MUSIC.

NAMES.	NAMES.
MISS EMMA ADAMS,	MISS LOUISA C. FORSTER,
MISS ELLA E. ANDERSON,	MISS MARY E. GARNER,
MISS AMANDA J. BARNETT,	MISS JEMMIE V. GATHINGS,
MISS SARAH A. BATTLE,	MISS SALLIE O. GILMER,
MISS MARY E. BATTS,	MISS LUCIA GRISWOLD,
MISS EMMALA S. BELLAMY,	MISS VALERIA GUNN,
MISS WILLIAM BELLAMY,	MISS TEXANNA L. HARDAWAY,
MISS M. LOUISA BONNELL,	MISS ANNA M. HAMMOND,
MISS MARY J. BRUTON,	MISS GRETA A. HAMMOND,
MISS REBECCA E. BRYAN,	MISS LOUISA E. HAMMOND,
MISS ROBA P. BRYAN,	MISS EVERETT B. HARRIS,
MISS CLARA B. BURTON,	MISS MARY A. HARRIS,
MISS ELLA L. BURTON,	MISS GABRIELLA HARRISON,
MISS CORNELIA E. CARSWELL,	MISS MARY A. HEARD,
MISS MATTIE A. CATER,	MISS SUSAN A. HOWARD,
MISS MARY E. CHAMBERS,	MISS MELINDA HUGHES,
MISS ANNA A. CHAPMAN,	MISS FANNIE R. JOHNSON
MISS S. CORA CLANTON,	MISS MARIA V. JULIEN,
MISS CLARA E. CLAPP,	MISS EMMA J. KENNON,
MISS HENRIETTA L. CLARK,	MISS MARIA J. KILPATRICK,
MISS SUSIE E. CLAYTON,	MISS SARAH E. KILPATRICK,
MISS MARY L. CONE,	MISS LIZZIE F. KING,
MISS EMMA C. CULLER,	MISS ELLA S. KING,
MISS VIRGINIA S. DOZIER,	MISS MARY E. LAMKIN,
MISS LILA S. EDWARDS,	MISS JULIA M. LESTER,
MISS ADDIE EVANS.	MISS SARAH E. LESTER,
MISS ANNIE P. EVANS,	MISS MARY E. LEWIS,
MISS URQUHART EVANS,	MISS AFNIE M. LINTON,
MISS ELLA A. EVANS,	MISS FRANCENA S. LOVE,
MISS JULIA A. EXPERIENCE,	MISS MARY LOVETT,
MISS OCTAVIA J. FENNEL,	MISS NANCY LOVETT,
MISS VIRGINIA C. FINLAYSON,	MISS MARTHA C. MARSHALL,

Ornamental Department.

------◆◆◆◆------

INSTRUMENTAL MUSIC—CONTINUED.

NAMES.

MISS JULIA E. MAUND,
MISS ELLA R. McKAY,
MISS LUCY McMULLEN,
MISS SALLIE MEACHAM,
MISS MARTHA J. MELL,
MISS VIRGINIA MILLER,
MISS SALLIE E. MOUGHON,
MISS MARY H. MUNNERLYN,
MISS ARCHER R. OGILVIE,
MISS AUGUSTA L. OGILVIE,
MISS LUDY M. PAINE,
MISS MARY W. PAINE,
MISS JULIA F. PELOT,
MISS SUSIE S. PERSONS,
MISS LUCY L. PETTUS,
MISS VIRGINIA E. POWELL,
MISS FANNIE E. PERKINS,
MISS JULIA M. PYLES,
MISS FLORIDA J. REDDING,
MISS ELIZABETH J. REED,
MISS JANIE S. REED,
MISS ELIZABETH M. REYNOLDS,
MISS MARY V. REYNOLDS,
MISS MARY F. RILEY,
MISS MARTHA S. ROBERTSON,
MISS SARAH C. ROBERTSON,
MISS SUSAN E. ROBISON,
MISS ANNIE D. ROSS,
MISS LEONA H. ROSS,
MISS MARY M. ROSS,
MISS MARTHA A. ROSSER,
MISS JOSEPHINE C. RUMPH,
MISS ANNA E. RUSH,
MISS SOPHRONIA RUSSELL,
MISS S. CAROLINE SEARCY,
MISS FANNIE M. SEARCY,

NAMES.

MISS ANNIE E. SHEWMAKE,
MISS MARY L. SHEWMAKE,
MISS ARABELLA L. SLAPPEY,
MISS MARY E. SLAPPEY,
MISS SARAH R. SLAPPEY,
MISS JULIA B. SMITH,
MISS MARY P. SMITH,
MISS M. FLORENCE SNIDER,
MISS GERTRUDE SNIDER,
MISS CORA C. SOLOMON,
MISS MARY F. SOLOMON,
MISS RACHEL L. SPAIN,
MISS EMMA L. STAPLER,
MISS E FLORINE STEVENS,
MISS OLIVE STEPHENS,
MISS CLEMENTINA L. STROZIER,
MISS CHARLOTTE E. TAYLOR,
MISS JULIA TAYLOR,
MISS CAROLINE M. TAYLOR,
MISS ELIZABETH H. THOMPSON,
MISS KITTIE TOOKE,
MISS ADALAIDE M. TUCKER,
MISS SARAH C. TURRENTINE,
MISS JULIA J. TURNBULL,
MISS EMMA J. TURNER,
MISS ELLEN V. TUTOR,
MISS EMMA WARD,
MISS MOLLIE A. WATTS,
MISS EMILY WHITE,
MISS ELIZABETH WILLIAMS,
MISS LAURA M. WILLIAMS,
MISS MARY W. WILLIAMS,
MISS VIRGINIA St. C. WILLSON,
MISS LAURA L. WIMBERLY,
MISS IRENE C. WOOLFOLK,
MISS MARY E. WYNN.

Ornamental Department.

DRAWING AND PAINTING.

NAMES.

MISS EMMA ADAMS,
MISS AMANDA J. BARNETT,
MISS LUSANNA BURGE,
MISS VIRGINIA C. FINLAYSON,
MISS LOUISA C. FORSTER,
MISS EVERETT B. HARRIS,
MISS GABIELLA HARRISON,
MISS SARAH E. HUDSON,
MISS FANNIE R. JOHNSON,
MISS FLORENCE JONES,
MISS SARAH V. LAMAR,
MISS MARY E. LEWIS,
MISS LAURA E. LEONARD,

NAMES.

MISS SALLIE MEACHAM,
MISS LUDY M. PAINE,
MISS MARY W. PAINE,
MISS ELIZABETH J. REED,
MISS JANIE S. REED,
MISS MARTHA A. ROSSER,
MISS ANNA E. RUSH,
MISS MARY E. SLAPPEY,
MISS EMMA L. STAPLER,
MISS E. FLORINE STEVENS,
MISS ELIZABETH H. THOMPSON,
MISS OPHELIA C. TUCKER.

ORNAMENTAL WORK.

NAMES.

MISS ELLA E. ANDERSON,
MISS VERONICA E. BALL,
MISS EMMALA S. BELLAMY,
MISS THEODOSIA H. EVERETT.
MISS MARY E. GARNEP,
MISS ELIZA J. HARRISON,
MISS ANNA HARGROVE,
MISS MELINDA HUGHES,
MISS MARY E. LAMKIN,
MISS VIRGINIA MILLER,

NAMES.

MISS VIRGINIA A. NELSON,
MISS LUDY M. PAINE,
MISS FLORIDA J. REDDING,
MISS ANNA E. SHEWMAKE,
MISS MOLLIE L. SHEWMAKE,
MISS RACHEL L. SPAIN,
MISS ELIZABETH H. THOMPSON.
MISS MOLLIE A. WATTS,
MISS EMILY WHITE,
MISS VIRGINIA St. C. WILLSON.

SUMMARY.

Senior Class, ... 19
Junior Class, ... 37
Sophomore Class, ... 52
Second Class, ... 39
First Class, ... 36
Irregulars, ... 21
Preparatory Department, ... 14

Total, ... 218

Instrumental Music, ... 136
Drawing and Painting, ... 25
Ornamental Work, ... 20

Total, ... 181

Course of Study.

PREPARATORY DEPARTMENT.

The studies pursued in this department are of an elementary character, but the utmost care is taken that in each individual case the foundation of an education is well laid. Each pupil is continued in these studies until such a degree of efficiency is acquired as to authorize admission into College Classes.

Reading,.. *Willson's Series.*
Spelling,.. *Parker & Watson.*
Writing,.. *O'Donnell's System.*
Scripture Questions,................................... *Summers'.*
Geography,.. *Mitchell's.*
Grammar,........................... *Clarke's, or Tower's Primary.*
Arithmetic,... *Robinson's.*
Composition Exercises,............................ *Brookfield's.*
Vocal Music.

COLLEGE CLASSES.

Candidates for admission into the First College Class must pass a strict examination in the following branches:

English Orthography—written.

Modern Geography—general outlines.

The Five Fundamental Rules of Arithmetic; and *English Grammar, through Etymology.*

The applicant must be able to read without hesitation, and to write a legible hand. If found deficient in any of the above, she can only be admitted into the Preparatory Department, where she will be retained until fully prepared for the College Course.

FIRST CLASS.

Orthography,........................*Smith's Gram. School Speller.*
Geography, reviewed,.................................*Pierson's.*
Arithmetic, through Percentage,....................*Robinson's.*
English Grammar,...........................*Clarke's or Tower's.*
The Bible,.................................*Emerson's Questions.*

SECOND CLASS.

Arithmetic, completed,...............................*Robinson's.*
Algebra,...*Robinson's.*
Structure of Sentences,.................................*Sill's.*
Rhetoric, commenced,.........................*Boyd's Composition.*
Latin, commenced,............................*Spencer's Lessons.*
The Bible,.................................*Emerson's Questions.*

SOPHOMORE CLASS.

Geometry,..*Davies' Legendre.*
Rhetoric, completed,........................*Coppee's, and Lectures.*
Latin, continued,................*Bullions' Grammar* and *Reader.*
Chemistry,....................*Johnston's Turner, and Lectures.*
Bible History,...................................*Hanna's.*

JUNIOR CLASS.

Trigonometry and Mensuration,........................*Loomis'.*
Latin, continued,............................*Cæsar and Cicero.*
French,.................................*Robertson's Method.*
Botany...*Gray's.*
Natural Philosophy,..............................*Olmsted's.*
Mental Philosophy,...............................*Haven's.*
The Bible.

SENIOR CLASS.

Astronomy,..*Olmsted's.*
Latin,...*Virgil.*
French,.......................................*Telemaque, &c.*
Physiology,......................................*Comings'.*
Geology,..*Emmons'.*
Logic,...*Whateley's.*
Moral Philosophy,.................................*Rivers'*
Evidences of Christianity,.......................*Alexander's.*

Exercises in Reading, Penmanship, Singing and Composition, are required throughout the entire course.

Instrumental Music, Drawing, Painting, and all other Ornamental Arts, are pursued at the option of parents, and in such a way as not to impede the progress of the pupil in the regular studies.

Two kinds of irregular students are recognized. First, young ladies come to the Institution whose previous schooling has not coincided with our course, but who desire to graduate. Their studies are adapted to their *status*, and, though temporarily irregular, they are brought to a regular standing in their class as soon as may be.

The other class of irregular students is composed of grown young ladies, who desire to spend a year or two in some good institution before quitting school. For such, the Faculty selects a course adapted to their individual cases, aiming, not at their graduation, but at doing the best for them under the circumstances. But while thus offering the privileges of the College to grown young ladies, the *Faculty protests against receiving girls to pursue an irregular course whose age will permit their remaining to graduate.* All our past experience demonstrates that such irregularity works badly for the pupil, and creates dissatisfaction towards the Institution. The College course is arranged with great care in reference to what society expects of educated women at the present day. It is the result of years of experience, and of consultation with liberal minded men. It is the constant study of the Faculty to produce *by it* the best possible results; a single irregular will give more trouble than many regular students, and with such results as satisfy neither teachers, pupils, nor patrons.

Collegiate Year--Vacation.

The Collegiate Year embraces a continuous period of about nine months and a half. This is divided into two terms. The first term begins on the first Monday in October, and ends on the last day of February. The second begins on the first day of March, and ends with the

ANNUAL EXAMINATION AND COMMENCEMENT.

The examination of Pupils in the Literary Department begins on the first Monday in July, and ends on the Thursday following.

The examination of Pupils in the Ornamental Department takes place on the second Monday in July, succeeded by the Junior and Sophomore Exhibitions and the regular Commencement Exercises on Tuesday and Wednesday.

There is thus but one Vacation in the year, extending from about the middle of July to the first Monday in October.

Literary Societies.

There are two Literary Societies, known as the Adelphean and Philomathean, which are composed of members of the College, and have increasing Libraries.

29

Fees.

REGULAR CHARGES.

Tuition, per annum, in Preparatory School,............ $40.00
Tuition, per annum, in College proper,.................... 60.00
Board, including Fuel, Lights and Washing,. 150.00

The only additional charges made to regular students are,

1st. Fuel, charged only to Day Scholars,.... .... $3.00
2d Incidentals in Matron's department.
3d. Books, when supplied at the College, amount variable in the different classes.
4th. Diploma-fee, paid on graduating,...................... 5.00

EXTRA CHARGES FOR OPTIONAL BRANCHES.

Tuition in Instrumental Music,.......................... $50.00
Use of Piano,................................$5 or 10.00
Use of Harp,.............................. ... . 10.00
Instruction in Drawing and Water-color Painting,.......... 25.00
Instruction in Oil Painting.................. .... 40.00
Instruction in Embroidery and Ornamental Needle-work,..... 25.00
Instruction in any Language but Latin and French,.......... 20.00

PAYMENTS.

All of the above fees must be paid in advance: *i. e.*, for the first term in October; for the second, in March. One month may be allowed for the payment of bills; *if not settled in that time, the pupil must be withdrawn.*

No pupil is admitted for a less time than to the end of the term in which she enters.

No pupil shall be allowed to advance with her class at the opening of the Collegiate year, unless all arrearages of money due for preceding years shall have been paid.

No candidate for graduation shall receive her diploma unless all amounts due the College shall have been paid.

Tuition is charged from the beginning of the month in which the pupil is admitted. Former pupils returning after the term opens, are charged for the whole term, if carried on with the same class.

No refunding of money paid for Board, unless the absence of the pupil exceeds one month : none for tuition, unless actual serious illness demand the removal of the pupil.

EXPENSES OF ROOM, DRESS, &c.

The sleeping apartments in the College Building are large and airy, each affording ample accommodation for four inmates. The heavy articles of furniture, such as bedsteads, mattresses, washstands, tables and chairs, are furnished by the Steward. The boarders are expected to furnish their own bed-clothing, towels, mirrors, pitchers, bowls, &c. An outlay of about $15, from each inmate, will amply furnish her with all needful comforts.*

Young ladies boarding in the Institution are not allowed to open accounts at stores, or to contract any debts. All necessary shopping is attended to for them, either by some of the officers or their ladies. All purchases are made for *cash*, which must, for this purpose, be deposited with the Treasurer of the Faculty, or furnished to the pupils themselves. Neatness and simplicity of dress are enjoined upon all. Parents and Guardians are requested to withhold from their daughters and wards the means of expensive dress.

---

* The following memorandum is inserted because it is so often asked. What articles should each pupil bring with her into her room? One pair Blankets, one pair of Sheets, one pair Pillow Cases, one upper Spread, one Mirror, one dozen Towels, one Broom, one Slop Tub, one Bowl and Pitcher, one pair of Over-Shoes, one Umbrella. For some of these, the expenses may be shared between two.

History.

THE public mind of the South was awakened to the subject of a higher education for females about the years 1835–40. As the first tangible result of that excitement, the Georgia Female College was opened to to the public in January, 18.9, under the Presidency of the Rev. (now Bishop) GEO. F. PIERCE, D. D. A few years after, by the opportune generosity of JAMES EVERETT, Esq., of Houston county, it became the property of the Georgia Annual Conference, and its name was changed to the Wesleyan Female College. At the period of its first going into operation, it was, so far as now known, the only institution organized with a full Faculty of Instruction, for the especial design of carrying young ladies through a prescribed curriculum of studies, on the completion of which they receive a literary degree. The liberality with which it has been patronized, and the rapidity with which it has been surrounded all over the Union, by flourishing and honorable competitors, evince the movement to have been demanded by the age and country. This steady patronage has enabled and prompted those in charge of the Institution gradually to elevate the standard of scholarship required in its matriculants and graduates, and affords gratifying proof of the public appreciation of sound and liberal female culture.

BUILDINGS.

The College Buildings occupy the front part of a large lot, on a hill overlooking the city of Macon, and surrounded by a number of elegant residences of families attracted to the locality by its remarkably salubrious climate. The main College Building is 160 feet long by 80 feet wide—the centre, four stories high, the wings, three. This Building contains 62 rooms, affording accommodations for the families of the President, three Professors, and Steward, and for 112 pupils, allowing for 14 Music Rooms, a Library, Parlors and Society Halls. The new Chapel is an elegant edifice, 90 by 56, with Recitation Rooms, Laboratory, and Study Room on the ground floor. In the rear of this, is the Study Room of the Preparatory Department, fitted up for about 80 pupils. There is also a spacious Dining Saloon in the rear of, and separate from the main building.

REGULATIONS.

The Officers, their families, and the boarding pupils, all partake at the same table, and constitute one large family, in which the supervision and care of the pupils devolves upon the President, assisted by his associates and the Steward, and their ladies. The harmonious and kindly feeling thus generated obviates the necessity of an excessively rigorous internal police. Confidence between pupils and officers is invited and secured.

The government is mild, but firm. The pupil is taught to respect herself, and to maintain the respect of others, by observing the proprieties of life in all her intercourse with them. The object is, first, to establish good principles, and then to teach her to govern herself according to those principles. To carry out this end most surely and fully, religion is inculcated as the best basis of character. Ample means are provided for the presentation of quickening truth to the mind and heart. The pupils are generally taken to church in the city on Sabbath morning, but when the weather forbids this, and on every Sabbath

33   E

night, religious services specially adapted to them, are held in the College Chapel. Besides these, which all are required to attend, there is a weekly prayer meeting free to any who may wish to be present, and three class meetings are held simultaneously in different rooms on every Saturday night. By a reference to the Course of Study, it will be seen that the Bible is studied as a regular text-book by every College class, and as much time devoted to it as to any other study. This prominence given to religion is thought to be no more than what is demanded of a church institution.

Besides the two small but rapidly increasing libraries of the Literary Societies, there is a copious College Library for the use of all. The philosophical and chemical apparatus is from time to time enlarged and improved by such additions as the advancing developments of science demand and afford.

Pupils boarding in the Institution are not allowed to receive visitors at the College, or to make visits out of the College, without specific instructions from parents or guardians, and even then, the Trustees require the Faculty to exercise a discretionary power.

Pupils are not permitted to visit, or receive visitors on the Sabbath, nor within the hours of study or recitation during the week.

The Faculty earnestly request and expect the co-operation of parents and guardians, in securing punctual and constant attendance upon College duties; nor will they consent to be held responsible for the mental improvement of any pupil who is prevented from attending regularly and punctually to all the required exercises of her class, or who is allowed to engage in such amusements or associations as divert the mind from study.

A report of each pupil's standing in her studies, attendance, and deportment in every respect, is sent to her parent or guardian at the end of the months of December, March and June.

All are required to pass the Annual Examinations in July, which are partly oral and partly written, but all conducted with great care, and under such circumstances as to afford a just criterion of the acquaintance of each pupil with her studies. These examinations are marked, and, together with the quarterly reports, recorded, and by this record it is determined whether the pupil shall rise with her class, or be returned to the same studies for another year.

Pupils are not allowed to receive boxes of cake, meats, or confections, sent to them from home. Fruits are the only eatables they are permitted to keep in their rooms.

Calendar for 1861.

—◆•••◆—

JULY 1st, 2d, 3d and 4th.—Annual Examination of Classes
    in Literary and Scientific Departments.
JULY, 5th.—Soldier's Aid Concert—8 o'clock, P. M.
JULY 7th.—Commencement Sermon, by Rev. J. O. A.
    CLARK, A. M.
JULY 8th.—Examination in Ornamental Department and
    Junior Exhibition.   Sophomore Exhibition at night.
JULY 8th.—Meeting of Board of Trustees.
JULY 9th and 10th.—Commencement Exercises.
JULY 9th.—Annual Concert—8 o'clock, P. M.
JULY 10th.—Annual Address, by Maj. F. W. CAPERS, A. M.
OCT. 7th.—Opening of next Annual Session.

Candidates for admission are urged to be present prompt-
ly at the opening, to be examined at once. Those coming
in afterwards cannot always be examined immediately, because the Professors are engaged.

Junior Exhibition.

WESLEYAN FEMALE COLLEGE,

Monday, July 8th, 1861.

~~~~~~~~~~

MACON:

S. ROSE & CO., PRINTERS,

1861.

EXERCISES.

Wesleyan Female College,

MONDAY, JULY 8, 1861.

"A name in the sand."

---

1. MUSIC.—Nathalie Waltzes............................Labitzky.
   Miss Stephens.   Miss Rumph.

2. COMPOSITION.—Socrates.
   Miss Octavia L. Fennel,....................Decatur, Ala.

3. COMPOSITION.—Winds.
   Miss Ellen V. Tutor,....................Vineville, Ga.

4. MUSIC.—La Ravel Polka....................Grobe.
   M. Rumph.

5. COMPOSITION.—Rome.
   Miss Sarah A. Lamar....................Macon, Ga.

6. COMPOSITION.—She Richly Endowed by The Creator.
   Miss Virginia Moore....................Savannah, Ga.
   Miss ....Slack.

8. COMPOSITION.—Gun.

Miss Mary T. Tindall,------------------------Macon. Ga.

9. COMPOSITION.—Men of the South.

Miss Sallie O. Gilmer,------,--------Montgomery, Ala.

10. MUSIC.—Romance—Veux-tu mon nom ?----------*Masini.*

Miss Reed.

11. COMPOSITION.—Ignatius Layola.

Miss Julia B. H. Smith,----------------Talbot Co.. Ga.

12. COMPOSITION.—Microscopic Researches. ✝

Miss Anna M. Hammond,----------------Edgefield, S. C.

13. MUSIC.—Var. Lucia Di Lammermoor Duett-----*Brunner*.

Miss Gilmer,   Miss Everett.

14. COMPOSITION.—Truth and its Triumphs.

Miss Laura E. Leonard,-------------------Talbotton, Ga.

15. COMPOSITION.—Nothing Great is Lightly Won. ✝

Miss Maria V. Julian,----------------------Macon, Ga.

16. MUSIC.—What are the wild waves saying ?

Miss Solomon.

BENEDICTION.

Sophomore Exhibition,

IN SELECT READING.

WESLEYAN FEMALE COLLEGE,

TUESDAY EVENING, JULY 9, 1861.

MACON:

B. ROSE & CO., PRINTERS.

1861.

EXERCISES.

Wesleyan Female College.

Monday Evening, July 8th, 1861.

"Oh popular applause! what heart of man
Is proof against thy sweet seducing charms?"

PRAYER.

1. CHORUS.—" Lo, the east with saffron tint."

2. SELECTION.—Authors—the undying benefactors of mankind. _____ *Whipple.*

   MISS VIRGINIA C. FINLAYSON, _____ Jefferson Co., Fla.

3. SELECTION.—A modern Cincinnatus. _____ *Anon.*

   MISS M. FLORENCE SNIDER, _____ Savannah, Ga.

4. CHORUS.—" Echo in the hollow glen."

5. SELECTION.—The moral world superior to the natural.
   _____ *Grimke.*

   MISS SALLIE C. ROBERTSON, _____ Greenville, Ga.

6. SELECTION.—Pride of Ancestry. _____ *Webster.*

   MISS GERTRUDE SNIDER, _____ Savannah, Ga.

7. CHORUS.—" Moonlight."

8. SELECTION.—Apostrophe to the Ocean,..........*Byron.*

Miss MARY H. MUNNERLYN,..............Decatur Co., Ga.

9. SELECTION.—Shaking Hands...................*Everett.*

Miss LILLIE A. WILLIAMS,.............Meriwether Co., Ga.

10. CHORUS.—"The golden sun sinks in the West."

11. SELECTION.—Letters.......................*Mitchell.*

Miss ADDIE M. TUCKER,.............St. Landry Parish, La.

12. SELECTION.—A curtain lecture of Mrs. Caudle...*Jerrold.*

Miss LUCY L. PETTUS,.....................Monticello, Fla.

13. MEDLEY.—Introducing "Dixie Land" and "God save the Queen" at the same time.

14. SELECTION.—Monument Mountain............*Bryant.*

Miss FLORIDA J. REDDING,.....................Macon, Ga.

15. SELECTION.—Memory and Hope............*Paulding.*

Miss SUSIE S. PERSONS,.....................Fort Valley, Ga.

16. CANTATA, by Preparatory Department.—The Graces; or Faith, Hope and Charity.

Fairy Queen—M. SMITH; *Hope*—MATTIE CHERRY; *Faith*—MARY BURKE; *Charity*—L. ROSS.

BENEDICTION.

Wesleyan Female College.

COMMENCEMENT.

FIRST DAY—JULY 9th, 1861.

MACON:

S. ROSE & CO., PRINTERS.

1861.

COMMENCEMENT EXERCISES,

Wesleyan Female College.

First Day—July 9th, 1861.

"'Tis hard to venture where our betters fail,.
Or lend fresh interest to a twice-told tale."—*Byron.*

PRAYER.

MUSIC.—Marcia by Wollenhaupt.

SALUTATORY.

Miss Catherine E. Cater,--------------------Vineville, Ga.

MUSIC.—" 'Tis sweet to be remembered."

COMPOSITIONS.

Miss Francena S. Love,-------------------Talbot Co., Ga.
Subject—*Georgia.*

Miss Caroline M. Taylor,----------------Pulaski Co., Ga.
Subject—*Cleopatra..*

Miss Martha Hoge,-------------------------Macon, Ga.
Subject—*Southern Literature.*

MUSIC.—The Love Chase.

COMPOSITIONS.

Miss Eunice A. Rylander,---------------Sumter Co., Ga.
Subject— *Old Age.*

Miss Martha S. Robertson,----------------Greenville, Ga.
Subject— *The Joys of Memory.*

Miss M. Lusanna Burge,------------------Newton Co., Ga.
Subject— *Greece.*—(excused.)

MUSIC.—The Fountain.

COMPOSITIONS.

Miss Amanda J. Barnett,----------------Milledgeville, Ga.
Subject— *The Advantages of Cities.*

Miss Ludy M. Paine,---------------------Aberdeen, Miss.
Subject— *Charleston.*

MUSIC.—The Impromptu.

COMPOSITIONS.

Miss Mary B. Johnson,----------------------Macon, Ga.
Subject— *Two Apples.*

Miss Sarah E. Hudson,------------------Jefferson Co., Ga.
Subject— *The Love of the Beautiful.*

MUSIC.—Jehovah's Praise.

BENEDICTION.

Wesleyan Female College:

COMMENCEMENT.

Second Day, July 10th, 1861.

MACON:

S. ROSE & CO., PRINTERS.

1861.

COMMENCEMENT EXERCISES.

Wesleyan Female College.

Second Day—July 10th, 1861.

———◆———

"Let us do our work as well,
Both the unseen and the seen,
Make the house where gods may dwell,
Beautiful, entire, and clean."—*Longfellow.*

———◆———

PRAYER.

HYMN.—"Heavenly Redeemer."

COMPOSITIONS.

Miss Emmala S. Bellamy,------------------Monticello, Fla.
Subject—**Victoria.**

Miss Josephine E. Rumph,----------------Houston Co., Ga.
Subject—**"Hope springs eternal in the human breast."**

Miss Catherine E. Cater,-----------------Vineville, Ga.
Subject—**Great Men as Types.**

CHORUS.—"The May Queen."

COMPOSITIONS.

Miss Meta M. Harbaum,-------------------Macon, Ga.

Subject—**The Present Age.**

Miss Anna M. Williamson,------------------Vineville, Ga.

Subject—**The Power of the Ideal.**

Miss Ophelia C. Tucker,----------------Laurens Co., Ga.

Subject—**The New Constellation.**

CHORUS.—"Grant to tyrant Kings their power."

VALEDICTORY.

Miss Ella Florine Stevens,------------Walthourville, Ga.

CHORUS.—"When the shadows falling."

CONFERRING DEGREES.

ADDRESS TO THE GRADUATING CLASS.

TERZETTO.—"Lift thine eyes!" from Elijah.

Literary Address
—BY—

Maj. F. W. CAPERS, A. M.

Grand Chorus.—"Should duty's voice invite us."

BENEDICTION.

ANNUAL CONCERT.

Wesleyan Female College.

Tuesday Evening, July 9th, 1861.

Journal and Messenger, Print.

PROGRAMME.

"There's sure no passion in the human soul
But finds its food in music."

PART I.

1. CHORUS.—Oh Hail us ye Free!................*Verdi.*
BY THE CLASS.

2. L'ELISIRE D'AMORE.—Duett...............*Wallace.*
MISSES BELLAMY, CATER, M. ROBERTSON, SOLOMON.

3. SMILES AND TEARS.—Song.................*Wesley.*
MISSES STEVENS and HARRISON.

4. WITCHES' DANCE.—Song..................*Wallace.*
MISSES REED and ROBERTSON.

5. THROUGH MEADOWS GREEN.—Song.......*C. Haas.*
MISS PAINE.

5. SEE ME NORMA.—Var...................*F. Hunten.*
MISSES REDDING and WILLIAMS.

7. HOME FROM OUR MOUNTAIN.—Song....*Il Trovatore.*
MISSES PAINE and SOLOMON.

PART II.

8. CHORUS.—Patriotic Song—"When tyranny contending."
BY THE CLASS.

9. MARCH OF THE NIGHT.................._Gottschalk._
Misses Bellamy and Paine.

10. "WHEN the SWALLOWS HOMEWARD FLY."–Song
Miss Turnbull.

11. I PURITANI.—Solo........................_Prudent._
Miss Paine.

12. GOLD-FEVER GALOP....................._Schulhoff._
Misses Everett and Persons.

13. TO OUR GALLANT SOUTHERN SOLDIERS.

Misses Gilmer,	Robertson,	Solomon,
Stevens,	Harrison,	Reed and
	Paine.	

SONG TO OUR GALLANT SOUTHERN SOLDIERS.

WORDS BY MISS M. E. CARLETON.

Air—_Marseilles Hymn._

Stars of the South ! we hail thy gleaming
Upon the ebon crest of night ;
For Freedom watched your steady beaming,
And kindled there your glorious light.
What clouds can dim your midnight splendor?
What noonday hide your peerless flame ?
In peace, in war, your light the same ;
Ye nations, see and homage render.

Chorus.—Then rise ! ye patriots, rise !
Your heritage defend !
'Tis Freedom arms you—on ye brave !
Be heroes in the strife !'

Land of the free ! shall tyrants rob thee
Of liberty, thy noble dower ?
Shall Southern braves to thraldom yield thee,
And in inglorious serfdom cower?

Our country's sire speaks from his ashes:
" Take down my sword approved by God,
And drive the invader from our sod
Once more, with battle's lightning flashes."

Chorus—Then rise ! ye patriots, rise ! &c.

Go patriots, light the torch of glory
Where Freedom's watchfires brightly burn ;
Go, re-enact your grandsires' story,
And _Southern_ independence earn.
We bid you God-speed !—soon returning
With victory's noblest laurels crowned,
A thousand hearts with joy will bound,
To welcome you, _our lion-hearted._

Chorus—Then rise ! ye patriots, rise ! &c.

SOLDIERS' CONCERT!

IN THE CHAPEL OF THE

Wesleyan Female College,

On Friday Evening, July 5th, 1861,

A SELECT CHOIR OF

FIFTY SINGERS,

FROM THE VARIOUS COLLEGE SINGING CLASSES,

Will perform the beautiful Operetta,

The Flower Queen!

FOT THE BENEFIT OF THE

Soldiers' Aid Society of Macon.

PERSONIFICATIONS:

Rose,	CORA SOLOMON.	Lilly,	S. GILMER.
Recluse,	V. LAMAR.	Hollyhock,	E. REED.
Sunflower,	J. TURNBULL.	Japonica,	S. ROBISON.
Crocus,	A. BARNETT.	Violet,	G. HARRISON.
Dahlia,	L. WIMBERLY.	Mignonette,	V. DOZIER.
Heliotrope,	E. BELLAMY.	Tulip,	M. HEARD.

—— o ——

HEATHER BELLS.

FANNIE BURKE,	LOU FOSTER.
LELIA SALISBURY,	LEONA ROSE.
LULIE BONNELL,	MARY BURKE.

CHORUS OF ALL THE FLOWERS.

Conductor, ... *Prof. Mathews.*

☞ Admittance, - - - Fifty Cents.

CONCERT TO COMMENCE AT EIGHT O'CLOCK.

Telegraph Steam Printing Press.

The Flower Queen!

OR

THE CORONATION OF THE ROSE.

A CANTATA, by Geo. F. Root --- Libretto by Miss Frances Jane Crosby.

[MISS CROSBY *is a Graduate of the New York Institution for the Blin l.*]

~ARGUMENT.~

THE Flowers meet in a secluded dell, in the forest, to choose their Queen. A person. dis-contented with the world, seeks, in the same place, retirement from its cares and disappoint-ments. The Flowers tell of love and duty; and the Recluse — learning that to fill well the station allotted by Providence, is to be happy — resolves to return again to usefulness and contentment among his fellow creatures.

PART FIRST.

No. 1,--INTRODUCTION.

No. 2,--CHORUS — We are the Flowers.

We are the flowers, the fair young flowers,
That come at the voice of Spring,
To deck with our beauty the sylvan bowers,
And perfume the zephyr's wing.

The blushing rose and the violet meek,
With the hue of the morn on its t mid cheek,
The dai-y that bl oms in the quiet dell.
The jessamine sweet and the heather bell;

The marigold, dahlia, and sunflower, too,
And the proud hollyhock with it gaudy hue,
The lily, whose home is the pensive spot,
Where it sighs to the gentle forget-me-not.

List! List! There's a footstep near!
Away! away! we must not linger here!
Hie we, then, to the forest shade,
And hide we all in our quiet shade —
    Away! away! away!

No. 3,--SONG: "Here would I rest, within this mossy dell," &c.—(*Recluse.*)

No. 4,--SEMI CHORUS OF FLOWERS.

Rest thee here, O. calmly-rest —
We will soothe thy throbbing breast;
And our sweet and airy numbers,
Stealing o'er thy tranquil slumbers,
Like the streamlet s gentle flow,
Shall beguile thy every woe.

RECLUSE, (*Recitative*)—
    Hark! hark! what sounds are those,
    So passing sweet?

FLOWERS--
    Rest thee here! —why should'st thou roam
    From our bright and blissful home?
    While amid young blossoms straying,

B lmy gales around thee playing.
Hope thy childhood's hours shall bring,
On her light and sportive wing.

RECLUSE —
    Again, their strange, mys'erious tones I hear,
    Like angel voices, stealing on the breeze.

FLOWERS—
    We will teach thee lessons sweet,
    In our cool and soft retreat;
    Here in one harmonious measure,
    Floats the artless song of pleasure;
    And contentment loves to dwell,
    In our green and mossy dell.

No. 5,--RECITATIVE—"Lost in wonder and with rapture filled," &c.—(*Recluse.*)

No. 6,--DUETT.—Wouldst thou know what sounds are stealing.—(*Rose & Lily.*)

No. 7,--SONG.—"O, gentle peace, with thy returning ray," &c.—(*Recluse.*)

No 8,--Chorus.

Who shall be queen --
Who shall be queen --
Who shall be queen of the flowers?

The summer is coming in beauty arrayed,
And bright bees are humming through forest
and glade;
O'er hill-top and mountain is merrily heard,
The voice of the fountain and song of the bird.

The fair'es are dancing o'er meadow and grove,
And pale stars are glancing like soft eyes of love
Then who shall be queen of our beautiful throng
--To join in our mirth and awake us to song?

We'll choose from the fairest that ever was seen,
And gems of the rarest shall circle our queen;
The morning shall linger the fragrance to sip,
Which the dewdrop hath left on her delicate lip.

No. 9,--Solo (*Crocus*) and Chorus.--"I am the first of all the flowers," &c.

No. 10,--Solo (*Dahlia*) and Chorus.--"Peace, false pretender."

No. 11,--Duett (*Heliotrope and Mignionette*) and Chorus.
'Tis not in beauty, alone, we may find
Purity, goodness and wisdom combined.

No. 12,--Solo (*Japonica*) and Chorus.--Prized by the beautiful and great.

No. 13,--Solo (*Sunflower*) and Chorus.
Chorus-- But who comes here? Who comes here?
'Tis the sunflower! 'Tis the sunflower!
Hail! Hail! Hail!
Solo -- Make way, ye silly praters, all, for me!

No. 14,--Chorus.

Say, where is our favorite lily?
The child of the peaceful vale;
The lily that bows so sweetly
It's head to the laughing gale?

Doth the dark-eyed violet linger,
Where cooling streams repose?
And where is the fairest and dearest--
Our beautiful blushing rose?

No. 15.--Duett.--(*Violet and Lily*)
Sister flowerets, we are here,
At your call we now appear.

No. 16.--Solo.--(*Rose and Chorus.*)
"The balmy odors which we bear,
And softly breathe o'r all the earth."

No. 17.--Recitative.--Lo! twilight shadows gather o'er the hills.--(*Tulip.*)

No. 18.--Chorus.

Come, come quickly away!
Soft winds chide our delay;
Night's call let us obey--come away;
Night, night, welcome to thee;
Our sleep gentle shall be;
Come, come happy and free, come away!

Hark! hark! softly and clear
Come away!
Sweet sounds steal on the ear;
Come away!, way!
Come quickly away, quickly away, quickly a-
Come, come quickly away, &c.

No. 20.--Duett.--Wherefore dost thou thus enchant me.--

(*Nightingale and Rose.*)

PART SECOND.

No. 21.--Chorus--(*Morning Song.*)

Good Morning!
Arise! The blush of morning bright,
Now tips the hills with rosy light,
O come, our sister flow'rets all,
List ye to the merry call.

Good Morning!
The night has kindly o'er us wept,
And watched us while we sweetly slept,
While, grateful for another day,
Hail we its returning ray.

No. 22.--Chorus.

To the choice, to the choice,
While the morn is blushing o'er us;

Haste to make our happy

4

No. 23.—RECITATIVE AND SONG—Softly, softly dear friends.—(*Ho*

No. 24.—SEMI-CHORUS.—We love you with true sincerity

No. 25.—SEMI-CHORUS—Stranger, thou hast heard our claim.-(*All the*

No. 26—A SONG.—'Tis hard to choose where nature's hand.—(*i*

No. 27.—CHORUS.

Prepare we for the festive scene,
We'll crown with joy our lovely Queen;
From rural cot and valley fair,
The purest, brightest gems we'll bear;

The bells shall ring their merry s c
And o'er the distant hills around,
Where sparkling fountains gently
Shall sweetly float our festive lay
Haste away !

No. 28.—CHORUS OF HEATHER BELLS.—We come from the hill

No. 29.—FULL CHORUS.—(*Coronation March.*)

We come from the palace in splendor arrayed,
We come from the mountain, the forest and glade,

We come from the cottage and green,
A Chaplet to place on the brow of
We come, we come, we come.

No. 30.—SEMI-CHORUS.—Receive thy crown, oh, Chief of Flow

No. 31,—SEMI-CHORUS.—On thy brow, the crown we place.

No. 32,—CHORUS AND ECHO.—

Long live our beauteous Queen,
 Bright be her reign.
Echo from rock to rock,
 Answers again
Long live our Queen.

In our united love,
 Changeless and free,

Here be thy greatest power
 Hail, hail to thee !

Long live our beauteous Queen,
 Honored and blest,
Peace be around thee still,
 Joy with the rest.
Long live our Queen !

No. 33.—SONG.—Filled with gratitude and love.—(*Rose.*)

No. 34—CHORUS.

We go to fulfill our glad mission on earth,
We praise the great being who gave us our birth
And lessons of meekness and love we impart,
As we whisper of hope to the desolate heart,
In the chamber of sorrow how oft we appear,
And our leaves are impearled with affection's warm tear,
We hush the sad moanings of sickness and pain
And restore to the cheek its bright blushes again,
We go, we go.

We smile in the palace, we bloom
And there is the dearest, the lovel
For we list to the prayers that a cend,
Where with contentment and inn
O'er the graves where the loved one's sleep,
We tenderly bow, and we silently
We'll eve~proclaim to the creatur
The goodness of Him who has give
We go, we go, we go.

No. 35.—DUETT.—I bless the hand that kindly led.—(*Rose and I*

No. 36. FINALE.—(*Rose, Recluse, Solos and Chorus.*)

CHORUS—

Light of eternal love, gently descending,
Pure from the throne above, mortals attending,
Guide thou his wandering way,
With thy celestial ray,
Where their enraptured lay,
Angels shall sing.

CHORUS—
 So may we each in different ways
 Our great and good Creator prais

CHORUS—
 Light of eternal day, guide thou his
 Where their enraptured lay Angel
 Softly we whisper, farewell, farew
 Farewell !

www.ingramcontent.com/pod-product-compliance
Lightning Source LLC
Chambersburg PA
CBHW021536270326
41930CB00008B/1274